ÐΛЯЌ ÎŊϸÎЯåŤÎØŊ Ц

GROTESQUE ILLUSTRATIONS, ART & DESIGN

First published and distributed by
viction:workshop ltd.

viction:ary™

viction:workshop ltd.
Unit C, 7/F, Seabright Plaza, 9-23 Shell Street,
North Point, Hong Kong
Url: www.victionary.com   Email: we@victionary.com
www.facebook.com/victionworkshop
www.twitter.com/victionary
www.weibo.com/victionary

Edited and produced by viction:ary

Concepts & art direction by Victor Cheung
Book design by viction:workshop ltd.
Cover image: Disco Ball by Amandine Urruty

ISBN 978-988-13204-7-6
Printed and bound in China

"THE THING THAT MAN ULTIMATELY FEAR OF IS CHANGE."

Alessandro Sicioldr Bianchi

People often describe my work as being disturbing and dark when in fact I would say my production leans more towards the sublime or the obscure as against the picturesque and the serene. The disparity between my intention and viewers' perception could seem obvious in the sense that there are no skulls, bones, blood, knives, or any other thing related to death or a lethal danger in my work. The figures that I create are frail and weak. Their gaze is not menacing, so why would they unsettle their viewers?

Fear of darkness buds out from the unknown. It is mystery that scares man.
Whether it be death, the dead of night or our incomprehensible unconsciousness, everything that
lies in the realm of uncertainty is linked to darkness. My images contain an unsolved mystery
which permeates my maiden's eyes. An inexpressible yet familiar sense of mystery reinforced by
their sweet and sad looks. A mysterious truth that no one can understand. Everything frail, mortal
and weak has a sinister side. The venous reticulum feebly pulsing below these characters' ephebic
pale skin makes the entire work disturbing and uncanny.

Darkness has a sublime beauty — not that kind of harmonious and sterile Renaissance grace but a
cursed charm that would bring about a forbidden, irresistible obsession. Incomprehensibly magnetic
are the signals coming from our subconscious through visions and hallucinations. Inexplicable is the
charm emanated from the caves and depths for explorers. And what about the endless dark chasms
of space for astronauts? What good is in the unknown? And why are we feverishly obsessed with
it? Perhaps because darkness is not only about journeying over to the unknown world of death, but
also birth and rebirth. Darkness exists in the wombs where embryos grow, the ugly and obscure
cocoons where caterpillars transform into butterflies and under the black earth where seeds sprout.
Every matter in our universe is undergoing an incessant movement of composition, decomposition
and transformation. Every single element that composes our system today represents the result of
countless number of disaggregation and aggregation in the past.

The thing that man ultimately fear of is change, although deep in our minds there are forces that
undeniably attract us to the universal tendency to transform, so even our bodies and minds tend to
move forward. Accepting this change means accepting death, and so be no longer frightened by it.
Perhaps this is why we fall so deeply for all the art that is unsettling and sublime.

Repulsion and attraction dance vaguely and ambiguously together in all the works of art
containing deep mysteries. They stimulate the human soul and lead us to confront with the
incomprehensible mysteries of the universe. Dark beauty is not characterised by the placid grace of
harmony. Instead, it is a melancholic choir speaking of unknown lands.

I often feel that my works are autonomous. Myths, dreams, fantasies are a complex of symbols
and images coming from the dark realms of my soul that only speak the "language of images" — a
tongue that we can't describe with our words nor understand with rationality. Even so, I feel the
need to extract and bring them to light from the chaos like a fisherman in a boat sailing in a dark
sea. The need of presenting them with a shape is my response to a charming voice — a calling
coming from my inner depth.

FOREWORD

The human condition has been a constant and central focus in many artists' careers. The torment of being enfolded by the unknown and the uncontrollable nature of life and death gives rise to powerful and intimate introspective subject matter and imagery.

To continue our existence our minds are highly dependent on our bodies and their intricate workings. The body has an ability to conceal potentially life-threatening problems while the active mind is reduced to being a spectator of our physical demise. The body is seen as a psychologically disconnected entity that is not entirely ours to control. Physical afflictions haunt our bodies and torment our minds by reminding us of our impermanence. The relationship between the mind and body parallels that of ourselves and our home where there is the symbolic association of safety, shelter and protection as well as the potential for it to be a site for trauma and damage. Our skin equates to the walls of a home, protecting us by actively separating the internal from the external environment. The house and the body are both palimpsests of life events where our personal history is inscribed into every surface. They are repositories of treasured moments, of everyday routines and memories, of growing up or growing old as well as being reminders of accidents, fears and trauma.

Where there is light there is always the potential for shadow. Throughout history, artists have magnified beauty and idealised reality and in doing so concealed the shadows. On the contrary artists who work within the shadows reveal the prevailing concerns of their time.

What exists in these shadows? You will find grotesque manifestations, the uncanny, the abject and perhaps even the surreal. The most intriguing artworks exist somewhere between light and shadow and are neither entirely negative nor positive. These artworks inspired by darkness are not always blatant or immediately evident because they often combine conflicting imagery and concepts. They can be compelling because they are not easy to discern and consequently the viewers' reactions are diverse. They sometimes utilise colourful illustrations or beautifully crafted objects to lure the viewer closer and then apprehend their gaze with a dark subject matter.

Perhaps an even darker concept is the impermanence of our natural surroundings upon which all life depends. Many artists strive to understand and connect to nature in order to clarify our existence and our purpose through the use of anthropomorphism and human-animal hybrids. There is also a prevailing concern for increased political tensions and the corresponding technological advancements in destructive forces in the name of warfare. War reduces life to an abstraction through impersonal and incomprehensible tallies of lost lives. For all the advancements we have made as a species we have disconnected ourselves from nature, the environment, each other and our inner selves, and in doing so we have jeopardised our collective and individual existences.

The artists featured in this book use visual imagery to confront the darkness that exists in our society in order to understand it, protest against it, challenge it, and revel in it.

Dark Inspiration is set to provoke and intrigue.

"THE MOST INTRIGUING ARTWORKS EXIST SOMEWHERE BETWEEN LIGHT AND SHADOW."

Fiona Roberts

"THIS BIG PARTY OF
BLACK IS MY TRIBUTE
TO ALL THOSE REAL
AND IMAGINARY
MONSTERS WHO HAVE
CROSSED MY PATH."

Amandine Urruty

I used to wonder why I love creepy things that much. But it's evident that darkness and fear are a crucial part of my everyday life all for one simple reason — I belong to the fervent clan who only watches horror movies. This passion is a family heritage, as my father used to do exactly the same. It was him who gave me the opportunity to experience my first chills and thrills at a very young age while watching *Suspiria* (1977), *The Funhouse* (1981) and *Re-animator* (1985). He used to be a "re-animator" himself and incidentally a huge fan of Rammstein and metal music. Every morning, you would see him wearing black.

The frequent presence of blood and guts had brought about a singularly curious environment for me to grow in. Every now and then, disgusting stories about amputations dominated our conversations at evening meals, and horrific books about skin diseases can be found casually laid on the coffee table.

Death, zombies and decapitations were good joke materials for my dad. I think it was his way to cope with the arduousness of his job. But at the same time they also turned me into a chicken. That's how I began my career, watching reports about serial killers and crimes of passion all day long, in my pyjamas. In a manner of speaking, Henry Lucas and John Wayne Gacy are my roommates.

Naturally, my fear of darkness, diseases, blood, and heights led me to become an artist, one of the most comfortable jobs in the world, and even more so when you work on your bed. However, my drawings used to be less dark than they are now, in every sense of the word. Colour can be a profession of faith, and black was my first unconditional love. Loud colours and rainbows arrived a bit later, as part of my "magical thinking" plan, a childish way to cope with a new and also a sad period I had to face. This immersion in candy pink and neon yellow lasted for two years, and led me to produce dozens of violently colourful pieces. When my dad died, I realised that these rainbow colours and magical plan were tragically useless.

Fiat lux! I don't need anything more than black right now. It is the golden thread that helps me create a visual bric-a-brac where all my memories, references and obsessions can go together, from Victorian post-mortem photography to Garbage Pail Kids, medieval bestiaries to dogs in Katy Perry costumes, and from *Sesame Street* to serial killer Jeffrey Dahmer.

This big party of "black" is my tribute to all those real and imaginary monsters who have crossed my path and my frivolous way to praise darkness. Here, Freddy Krueger plays records, and Joseph Merrick shows us how to dance.

In hindsight, now I can admit that my artistic progress has embraced these two main things which used to be my father's areas of interest: death and jokes, among skeletons and Whoopie Cushions, ghosts, blood, and boogers. Let's laugh a bit before we die, he would have said.

And draw a big dance of death led by sausages.

Was?!

KRAKKS

Fig. 2.

Okt. 1904.   Jan. 1904.

The Bloody Gardener's Cruelty;
Or, The Shepherd's Daughter Betray'd.

The youthful shepherdess of this nothing knew,
But went to meet her true love as she used to do;
She search'd the garden all around, but no true love she found.
At length the Bloody Gardener did appear.

What business have you here, madam, I pray?
Are you come here to rob the garden gay?
Cries she, No thief I am, but wait for that young-man,
Who did this night appoint to meet me here.

He spoke no more, but strait a knife he took,
And pierc'd her heart before one word she spoke,
Then on the ground she fell, crying, Sweet love, farewell.
O welcome, welcome, Death, thy fatal stroke.

Was this done now, my dear; by your design?
Or by your cruel parents most unkind,
My life is thus betray'd?—farewell vain world, she said,
I hope in heaven I a place shall find

But when he see her life was really gone,
Immediately he lay'd her in the ground,
With flowers fine and gay her corpse did overlay,
Intending that her body should not be found.

[Excerpt]

The Twa Sisters

There were two sisters, they went playing,
Refrain: With a hie downe downe a downe-a
To see their father's ships come sayling in.
Refrain: With a hy downe downe a downe-a
And when they came unto the sea-brym,
The elder did push the younger in.

'O sister, O sister, take me by the gowne,
And drawe me up upon the dry ground.'
'O sister, O sister, that may not bee,
Till salt and oatmeale grow both of a tree.'

Somtymes she sanke, somtymes she swam,
Until she came unto the mill-dam.
The miller runne hastily downe the cliffe,
And up he betook her withouten her life.

What did he doe with her brest-bone?
He made him a violl to play thereupon.
What did he doe with her fingers so small?
He made him peggs to his violl withall.

What did he doe with her nose-ridge?
Unto his violl he made him a bridge.
What did he doe with her veynes so blew?
He made him strings to his violl thereto.

What did he doe with her eyes so bright?
Upon his violl he played at first sight.
What did he doe with her tongue so rough?
Unto the violl it spake enough.
What did he doe with her two shinnes?
Unto the violl they danc'd Moll Syms.

Then bespake the treble string,
'O yonder is my father the king.'
Then bespake the second string,
'O yonder sitts my mother the queen.'
And then bespake the strings all three,
'O yonder is my sister that drowned mee.'
'Now pay the miller for his payne,
And let him bee gone in the divel's name.'

024

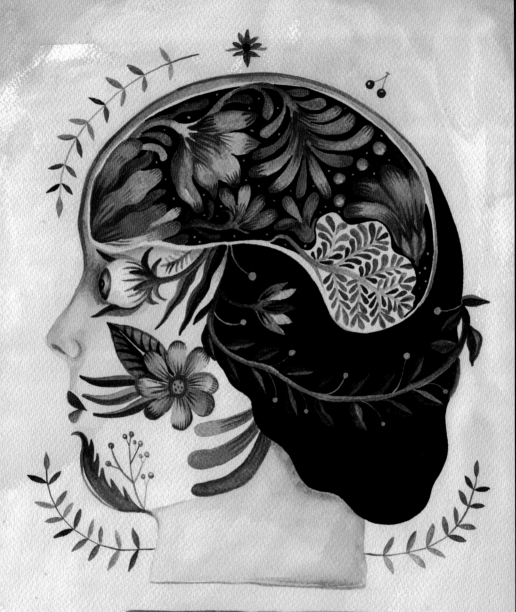

HEAD

F O O T   H A N D

HUMAN

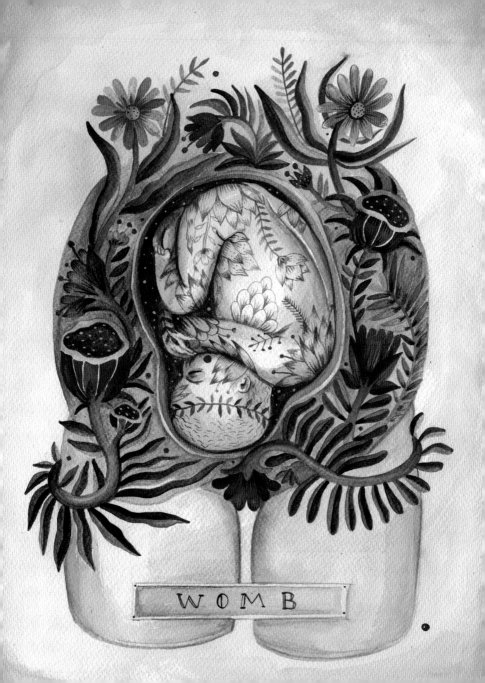

WOMB

SKELETON

SKULL

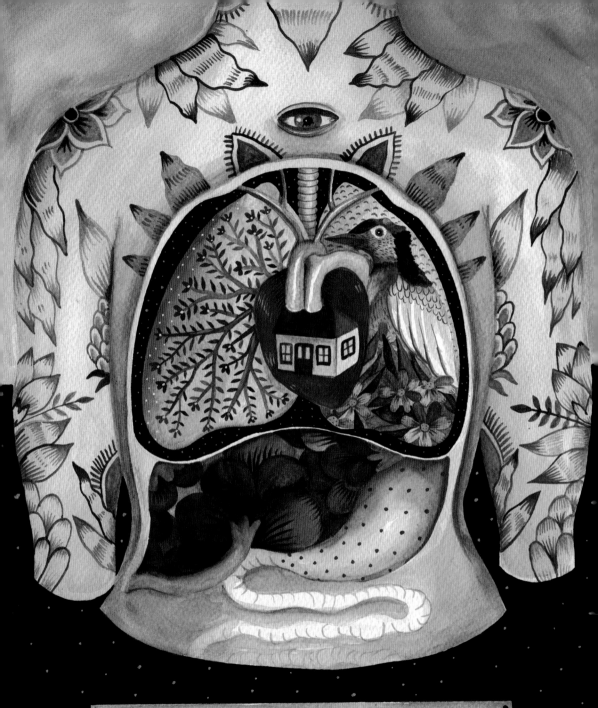

CHEST & ABDOMEN

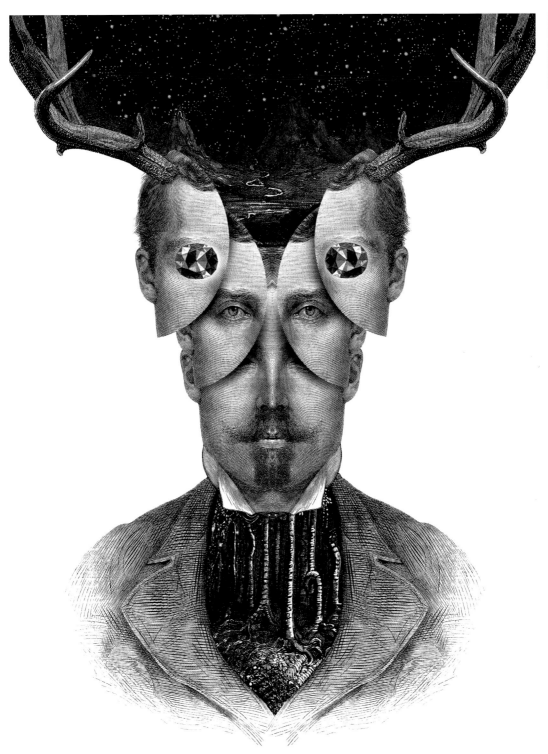

049

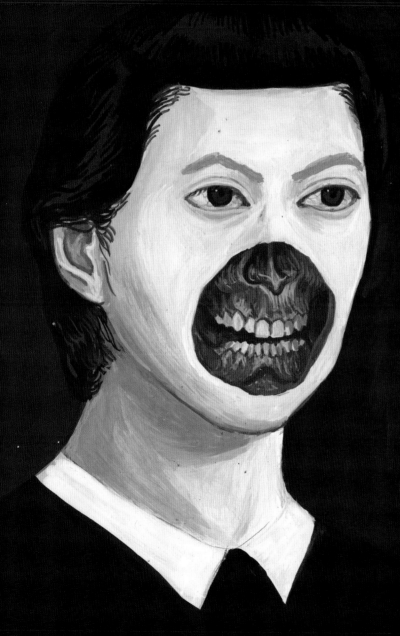

DADU SHIN

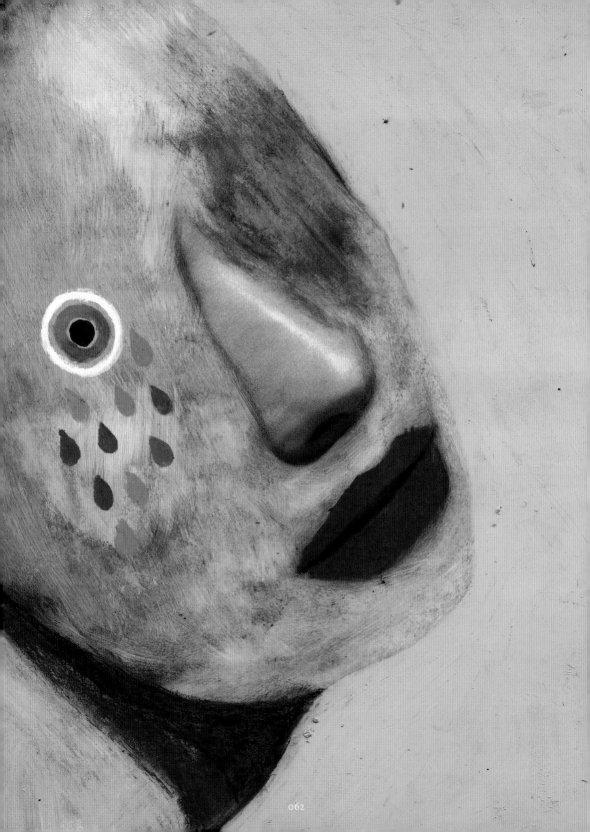

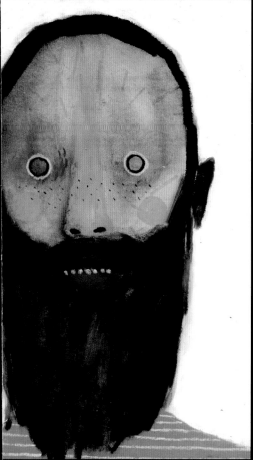

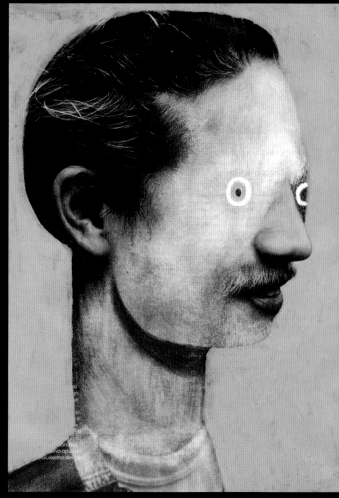

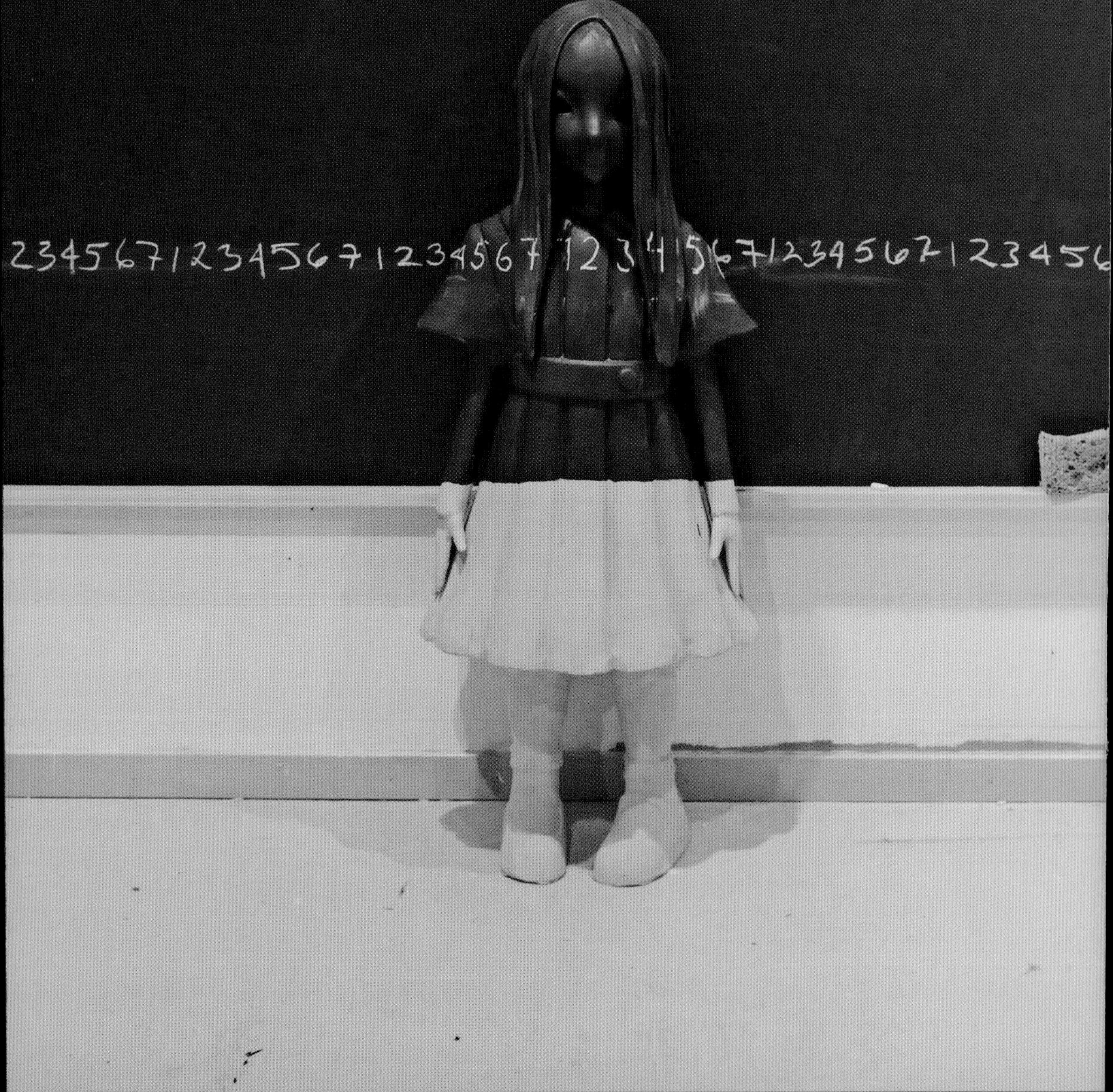

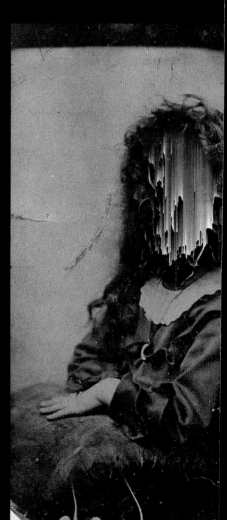

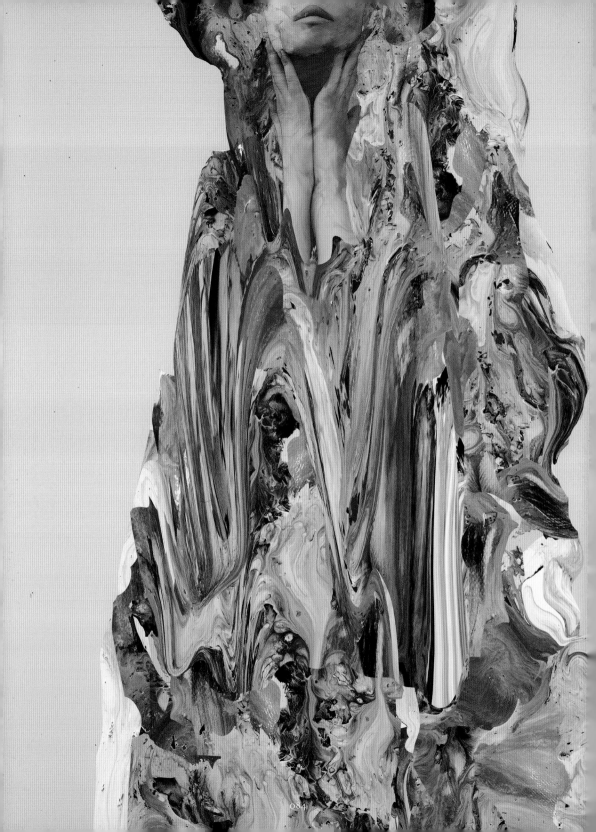

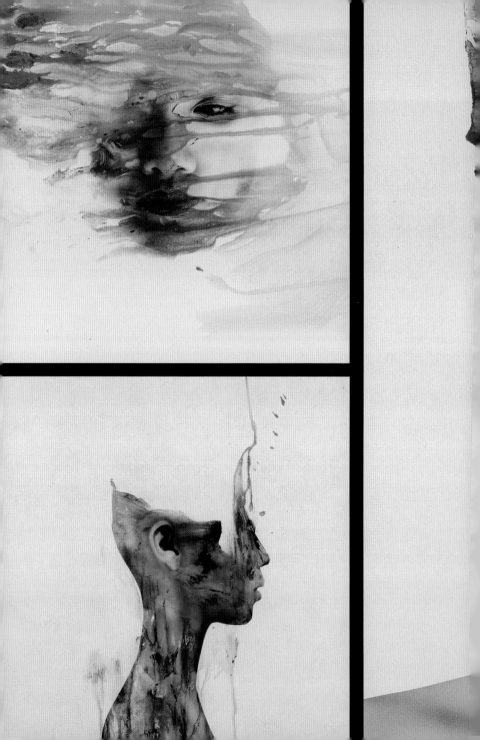

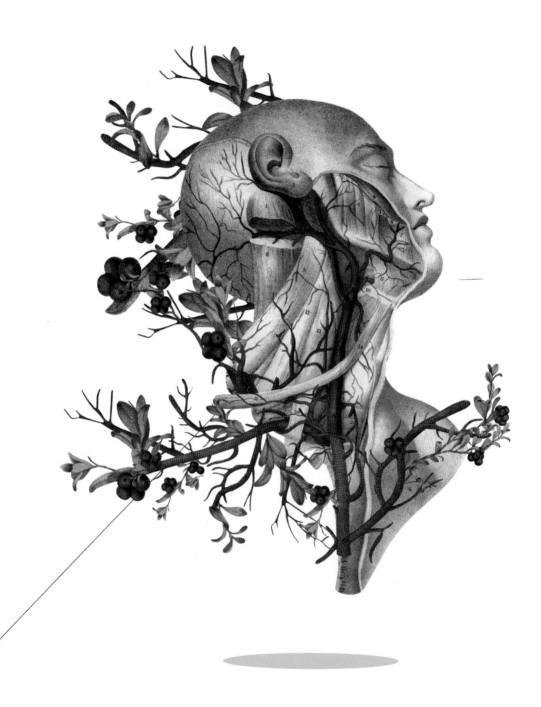

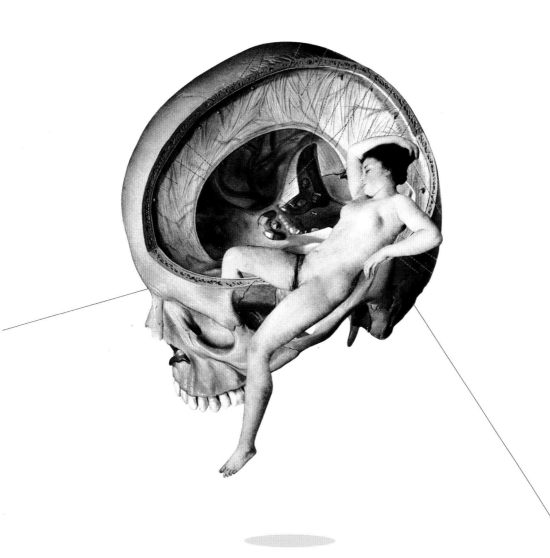

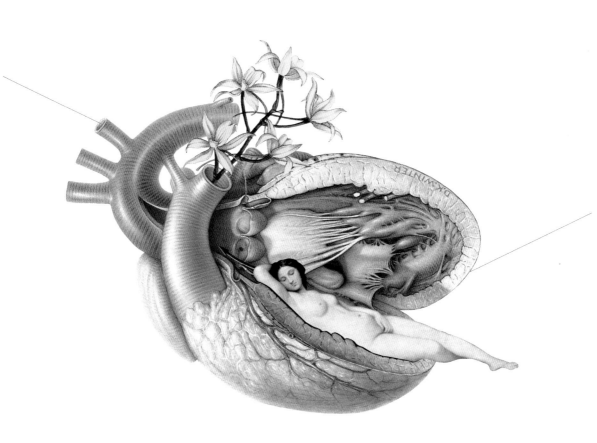

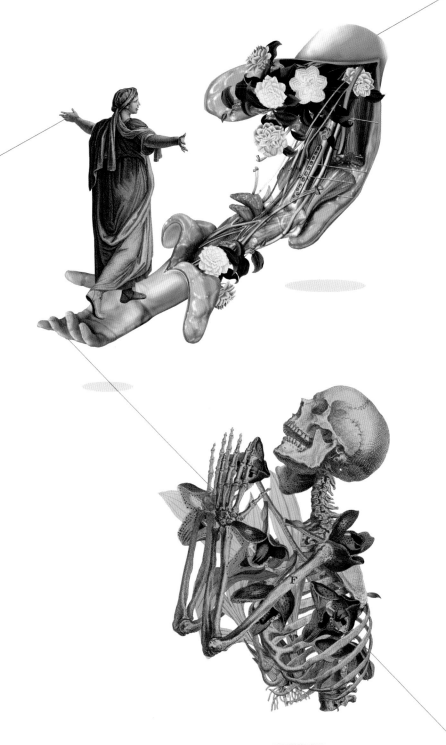

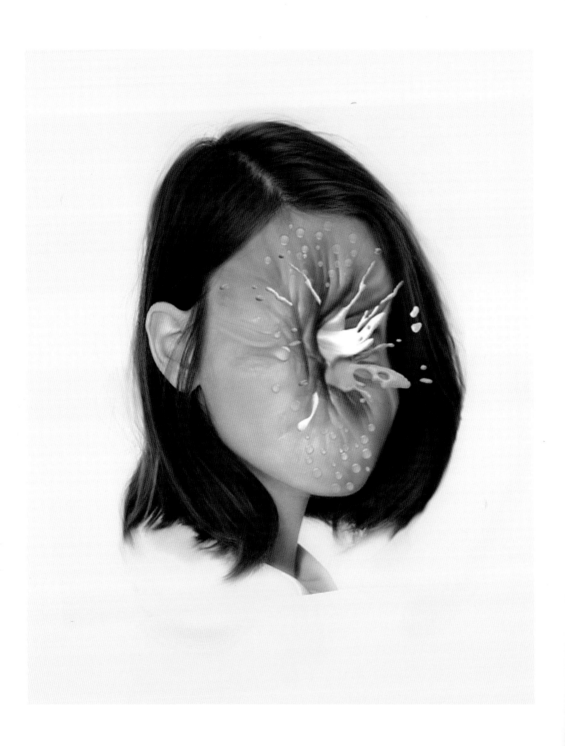

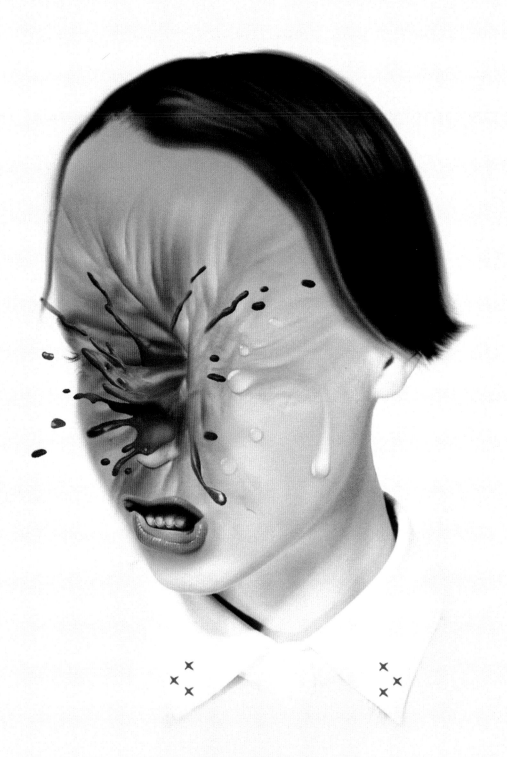

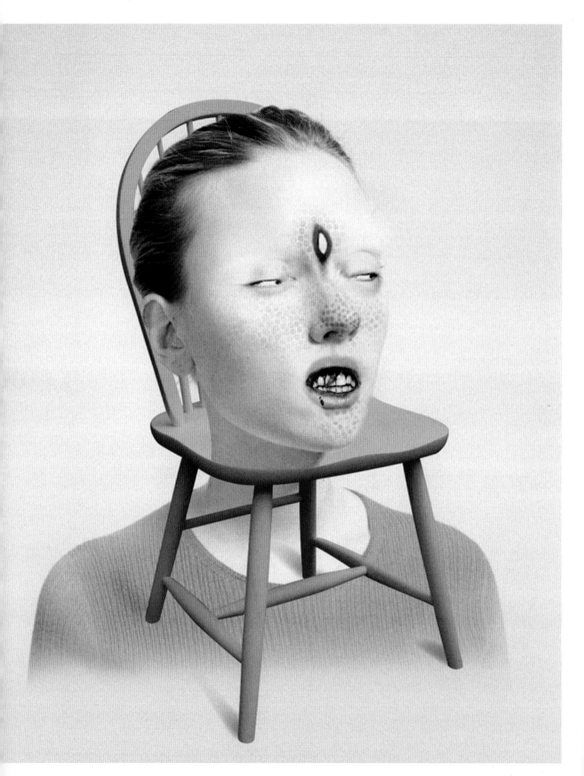

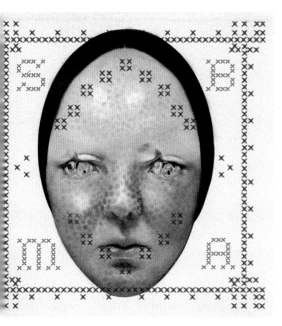

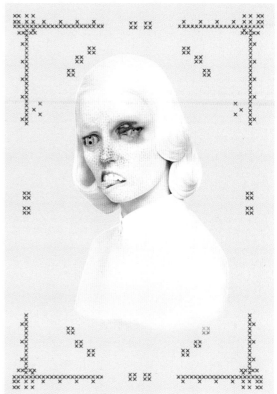

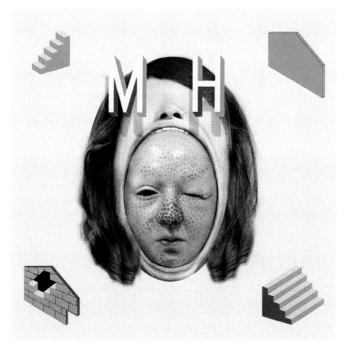

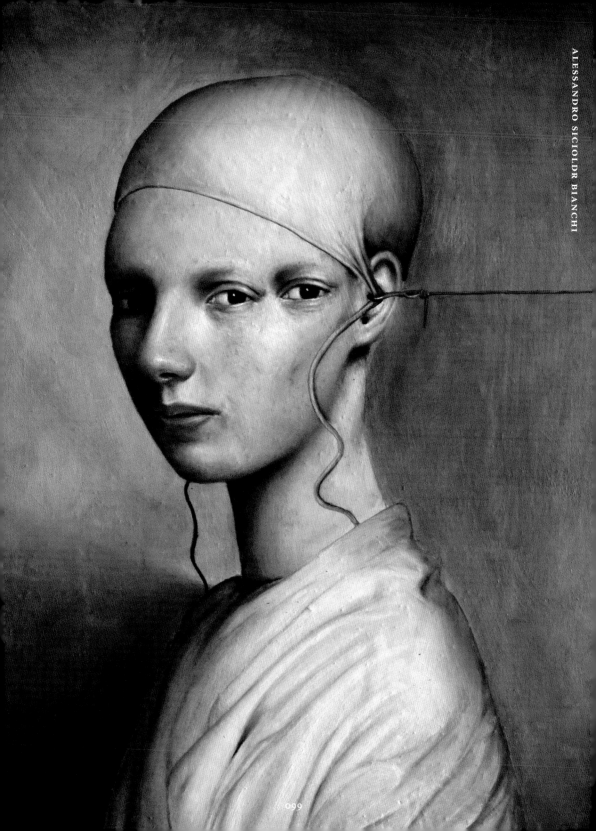

The irresponsive silence of the land,
The irresponsive sounding of the sea,
Speak both one message of one sense to me:—
Aloof, aloof, we stand aloof, so stand
Thou too aloof bound with the flawless band
Of inner solitude; we bind not thee;
But who from thy self-chain shall set thee free?
What heart shall touch thy heart? what hand thy hand?—
And I am sometimes proud and sometimes meek,
And sometimes I remember days of old
When fellowship seemed not so far to seek
And all the world and I seemed much less cold,
And at the rainbow's foot lay surely gold,
And hope felt strong and life itself not weak.

Thus am I mine own prison. Everything
Around me free and sunny and at ease:
Or if in shadow, in a shade of trees
Which the sun kisses, where the gay birds sing
And where all winds make various murmuring;
Where bees are found, with honey for the bees;
Where sounds are music, and where silences
Are music of an unlike fashioning.

Then gaze I at the merrymaking crew,
And smile a moment and a moment sigh
Thinking: Why can I not rejoice with you?
But soon I put the foolish fancy by:
I am not what I have nor what I do;
But what I was I am, I am even I.

Therefore myself is that one only thing
I hold to use or waste, to keep or give;
My sole possession every day I live,
And still mine own despite Time's winnowing.
Ever mine own, while moons and seasons bring
From crudeness ripeness mellow and sanative;
Ever mine own, till Death shall ply his sieve;
And still mine own, when saints break grave and sing.
And this myself as king unto my King
I give, to Him Who gave Himself for me;
Who gives Himself to me, and bids me sing
A sweet new song of His redeemed set free;
He bids me sing: O death, where is thy sting?
And sing: O grave, where is thy victory?

The Thread of Life
— Christina Rossetti

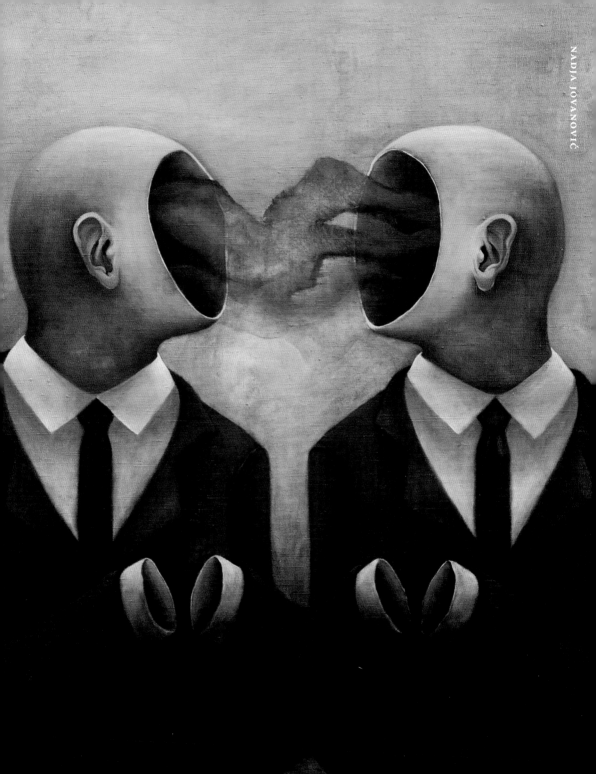

IGNIS

TERRA

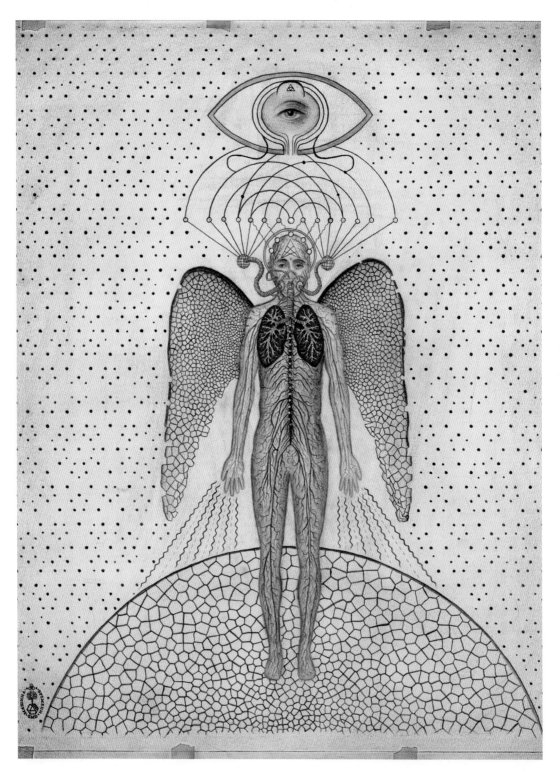

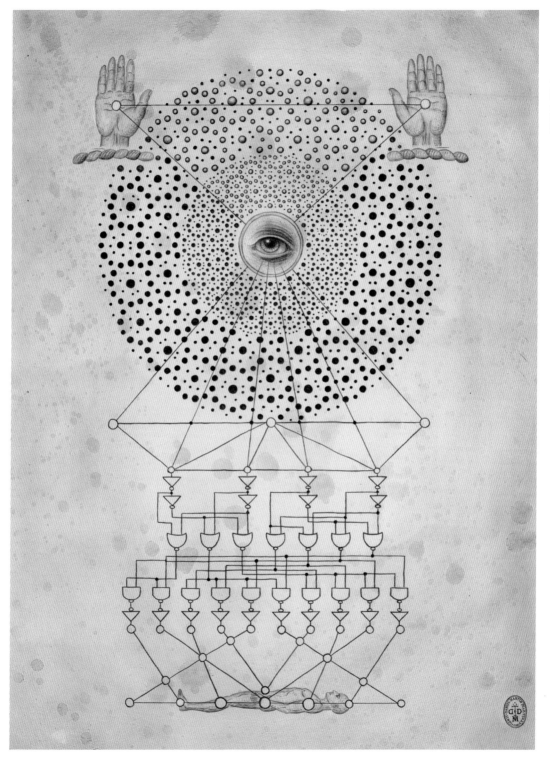

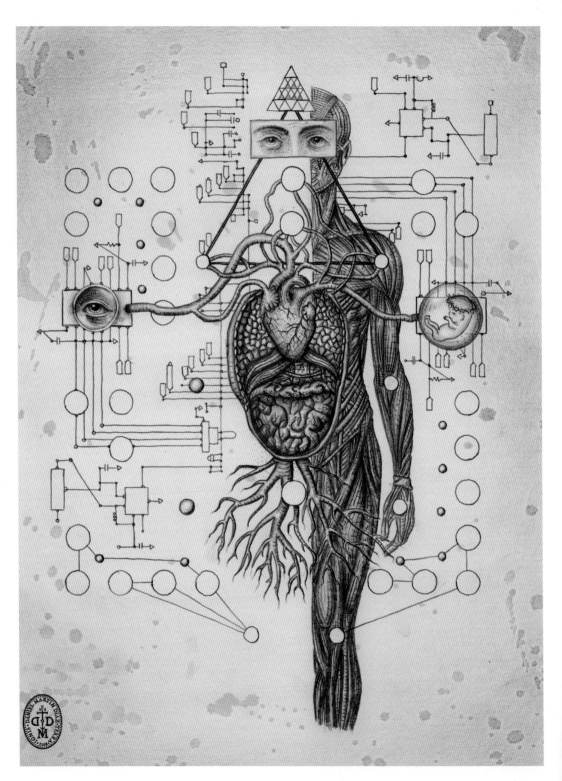

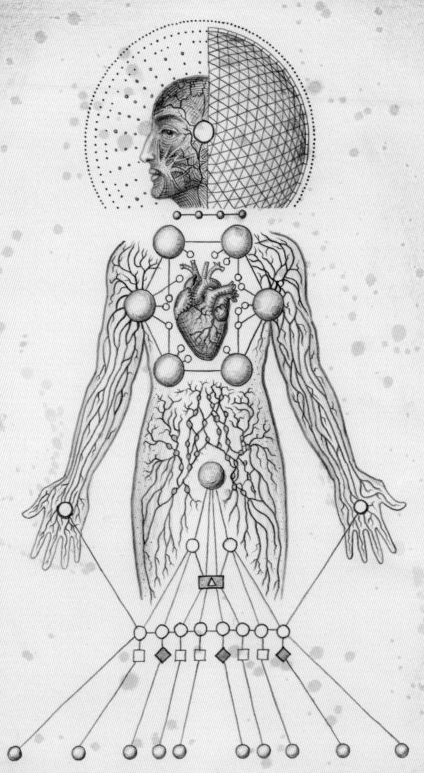

01001101 11101110 11001101

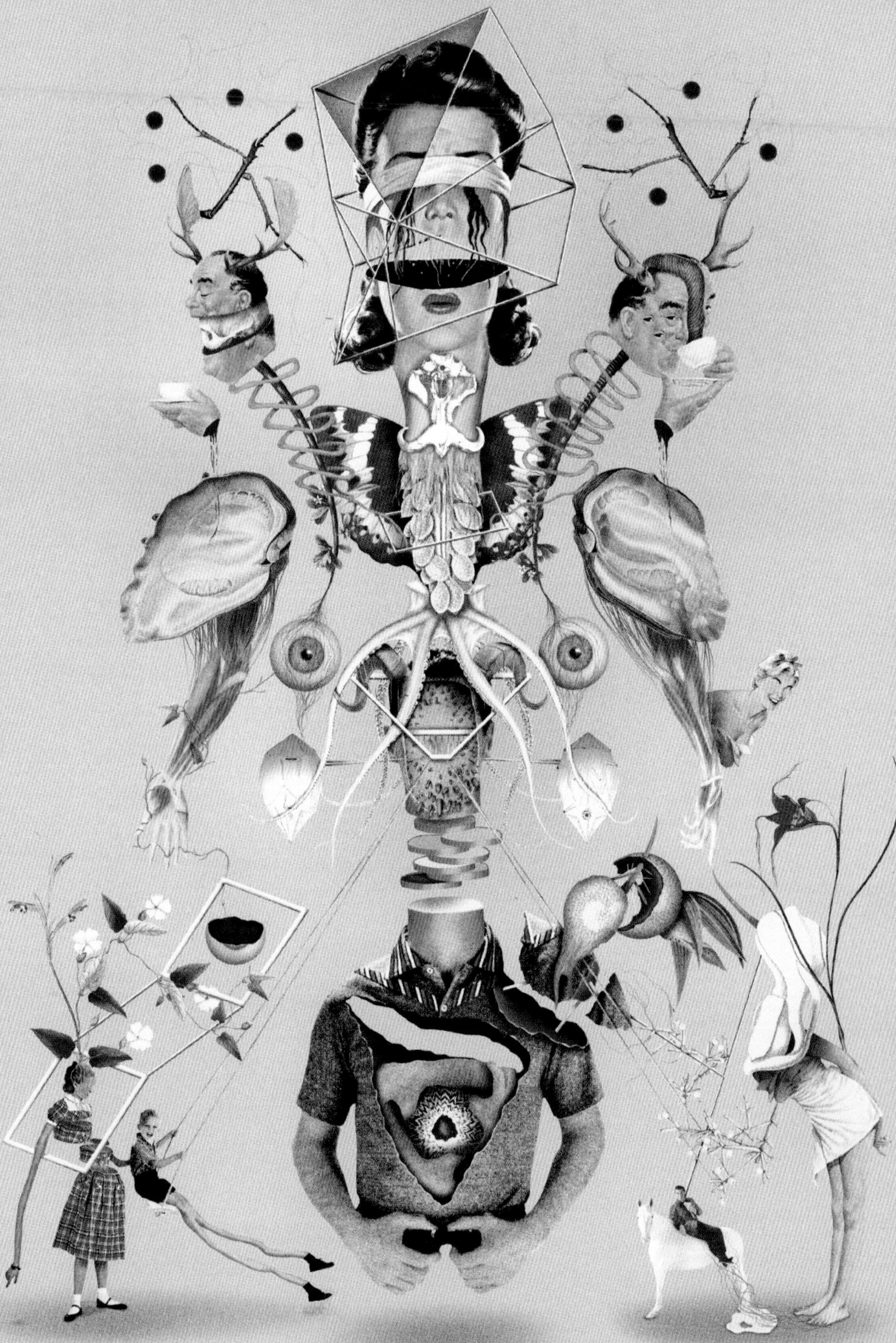

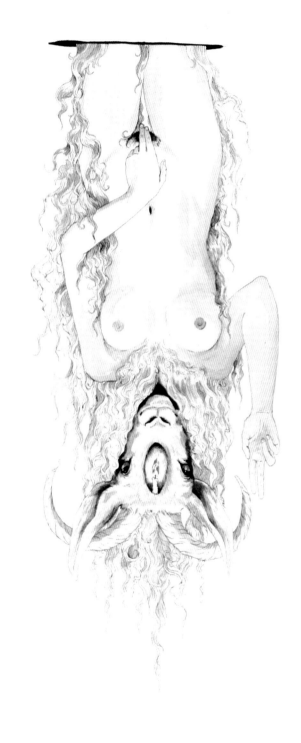

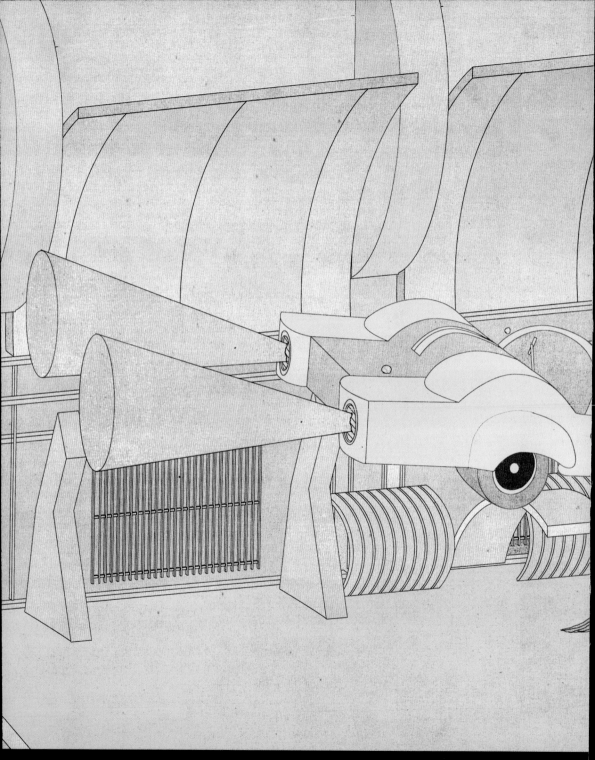

KOTARO CHIBA

KOTARO CHIBA

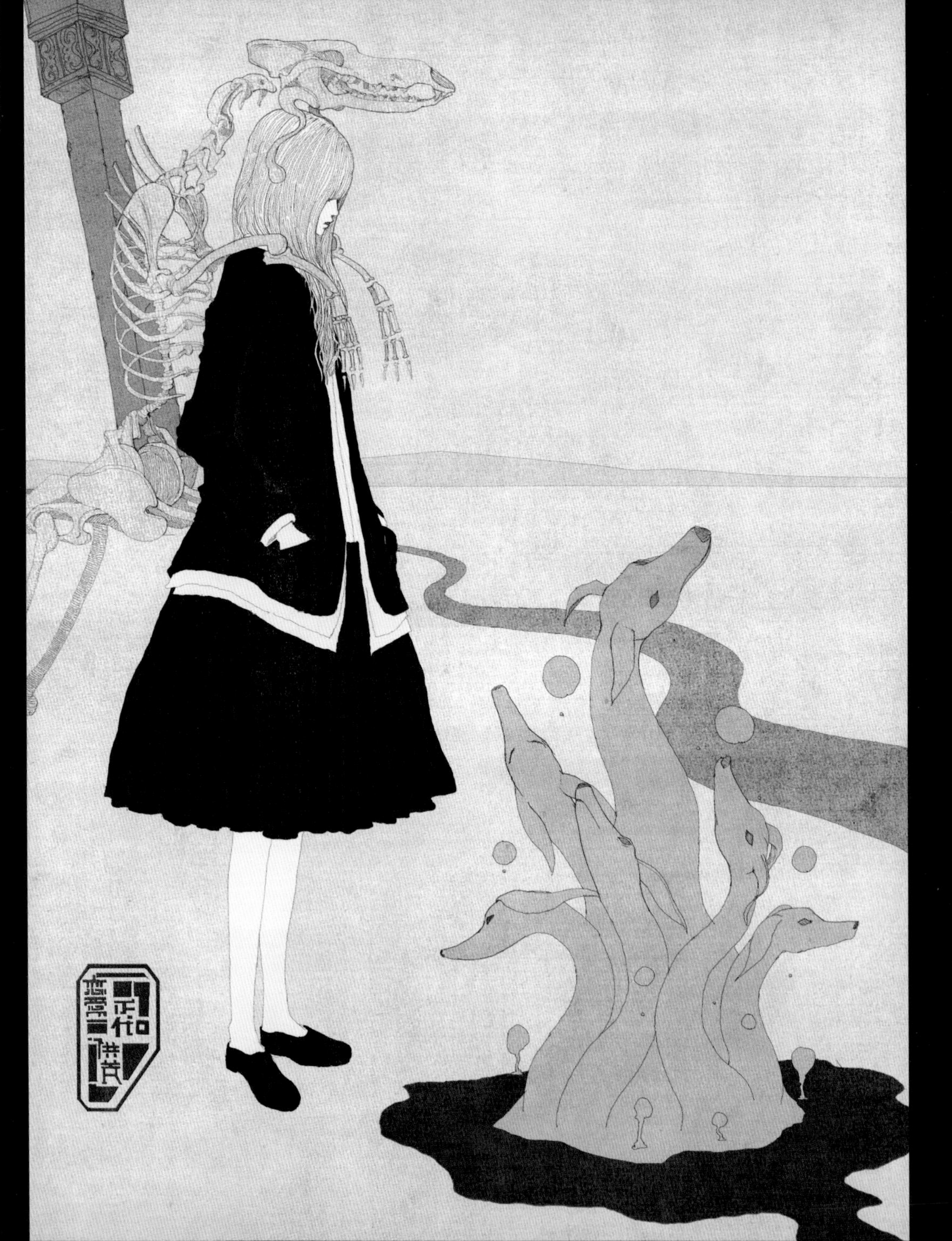

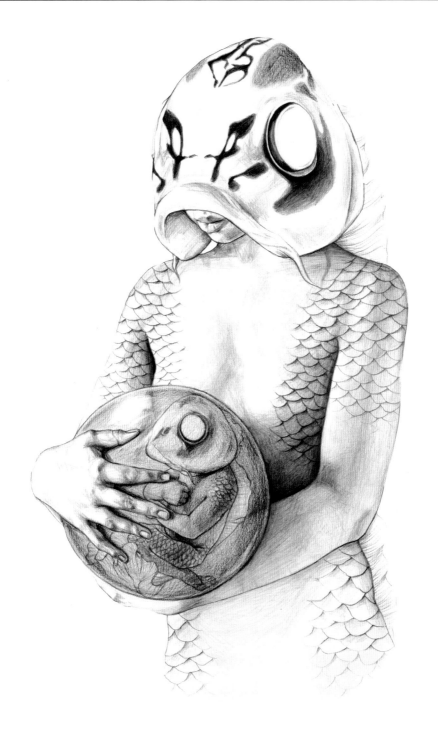

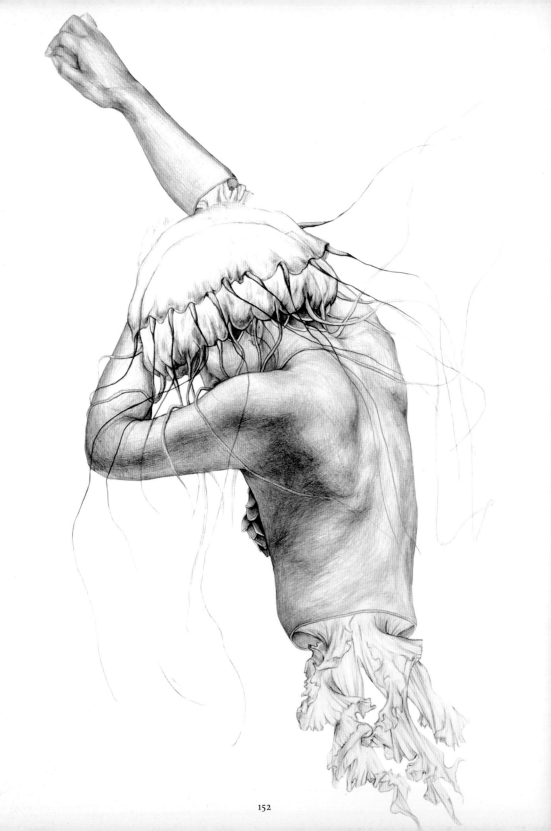

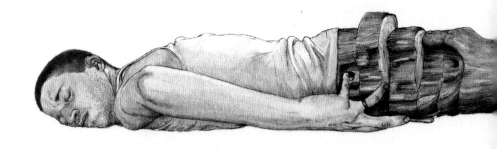

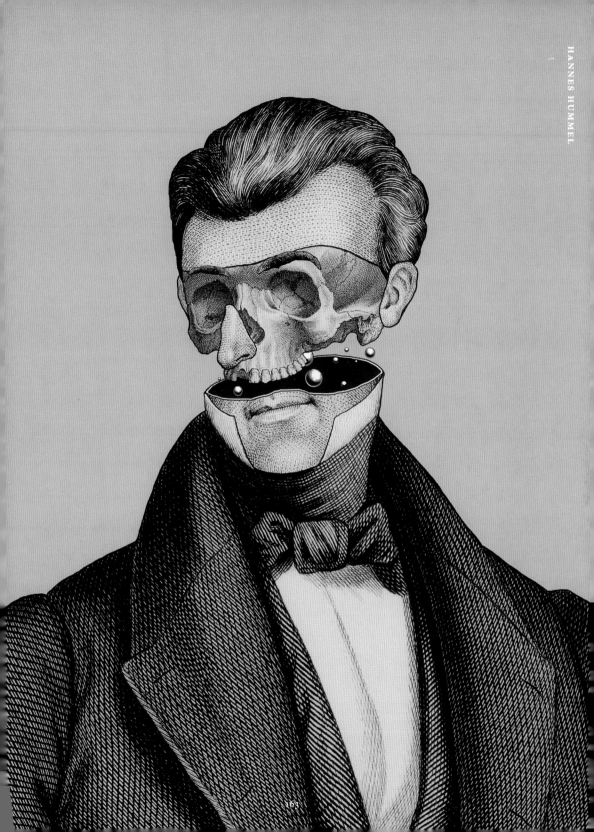

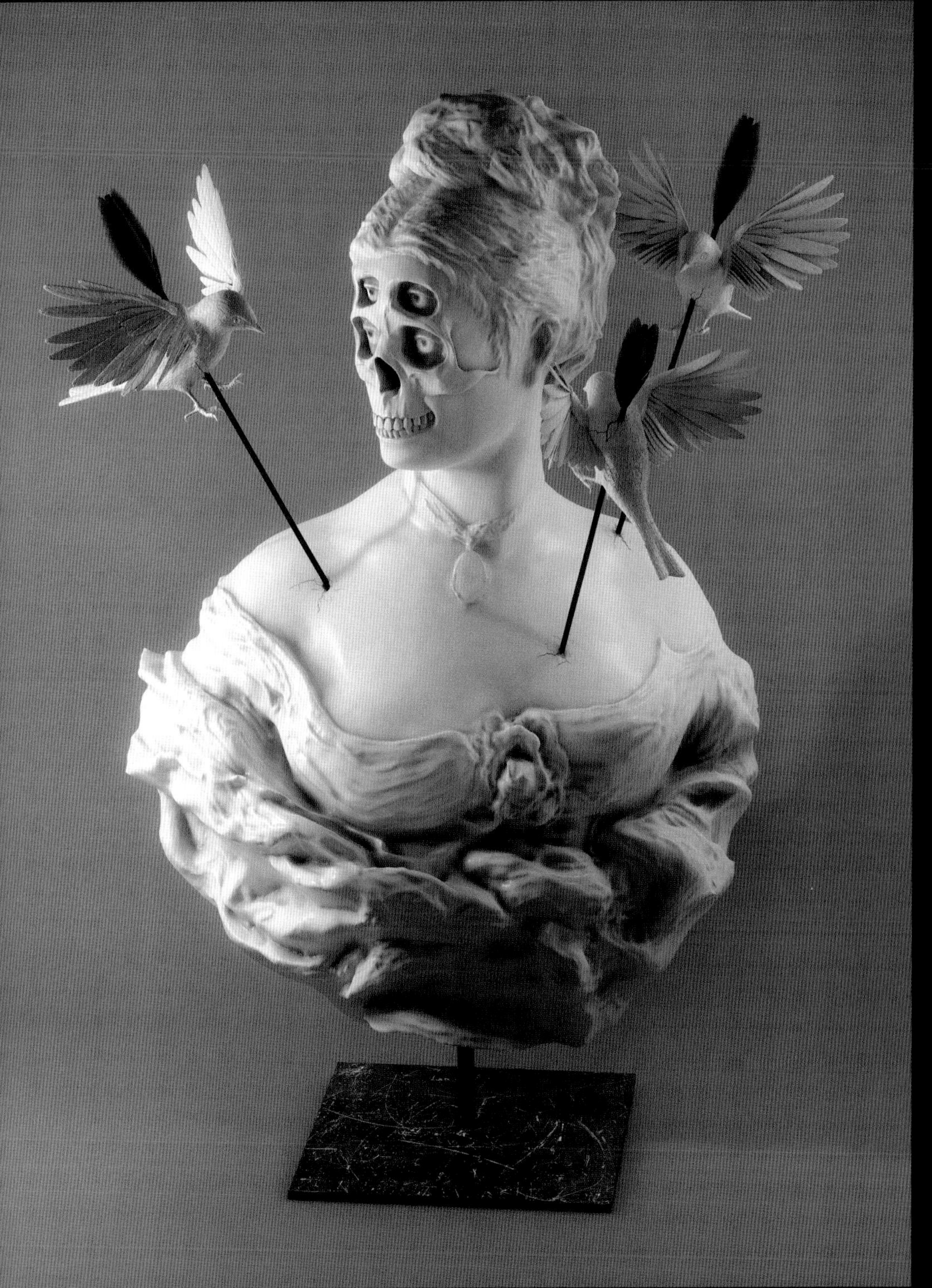

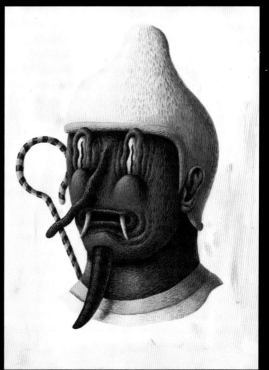

Prepare, prepare, new guests draw near,
And on the brink of hell appear.

Kindle fresh flames of sulphur there.
        Assemble all ye fiends,
        Wait for the dreadful ends
Of impious men, who far excel
        All th' inhabitants of hell.

        Let 'em come, let 'em come,
To an eternal dreadful doom,
        Let 'em come, let 'em come.

In mischiefs they have all the damned outdone;
Here they shall weep, and shall unpitied groan,
Here they shall howl, and make eternal moan.

By blood and lust they have deserved so well,
That they shall feel the hottest flames of hell.

In vain they shall here their past mischiefs bew

Eternal darkness they shall find,
        And them eternal chains shall bind
        To infinite pain of sense and mind.

        Let 'em come, let 'em come,
To an eternal dreadful doom,
        Let 'em come, let 'em come.

Song of Devils
— *Thomas Shadwell*

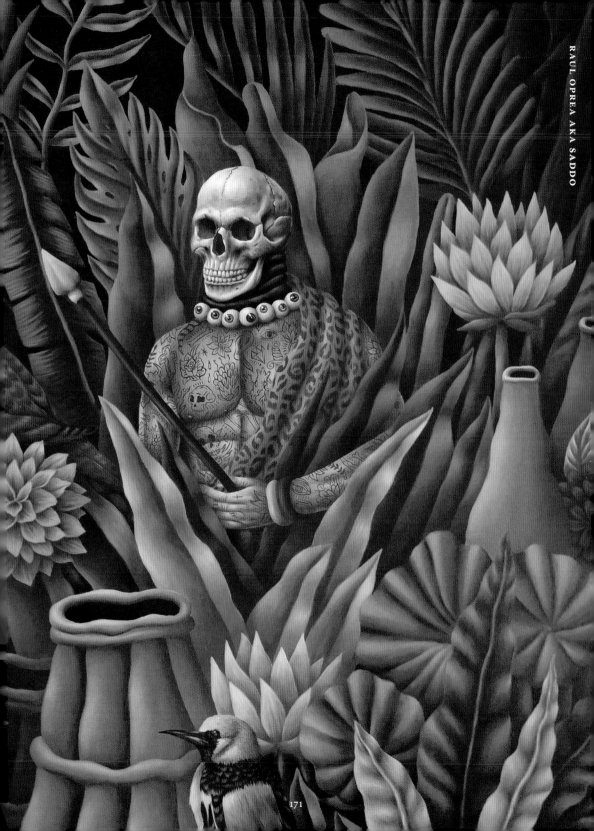

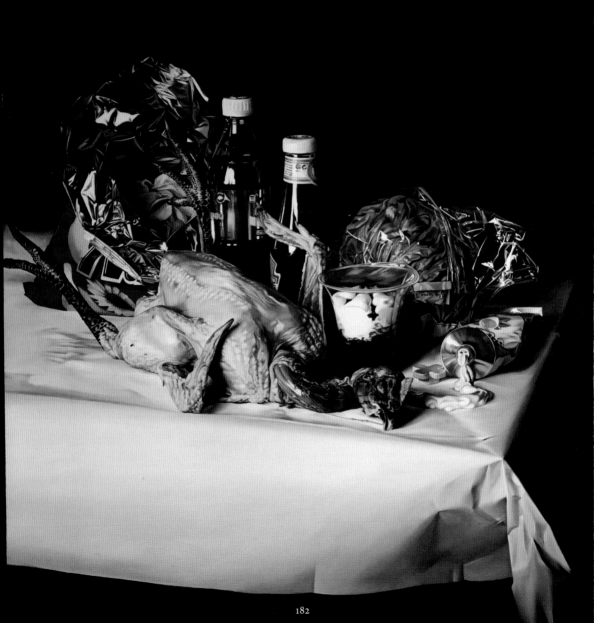

190°

ci.

clo.

sis.

ge.

ne.

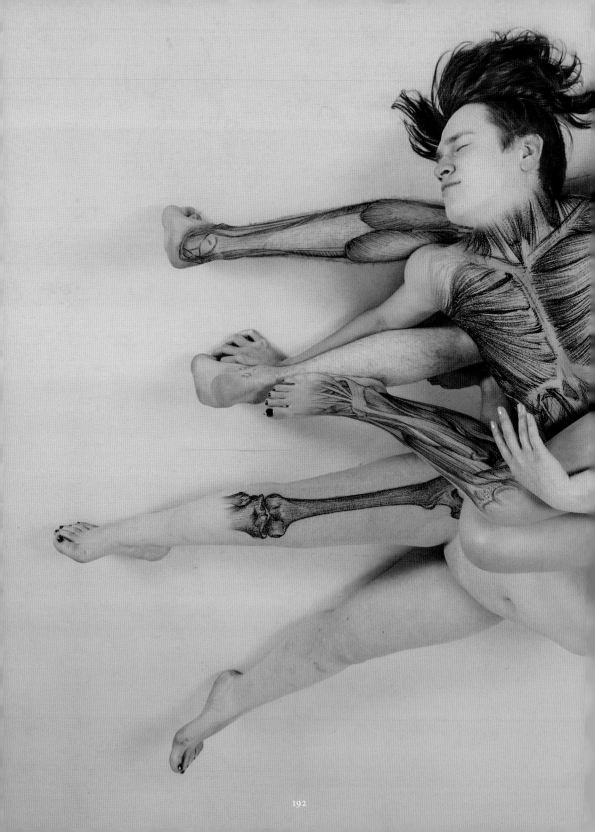

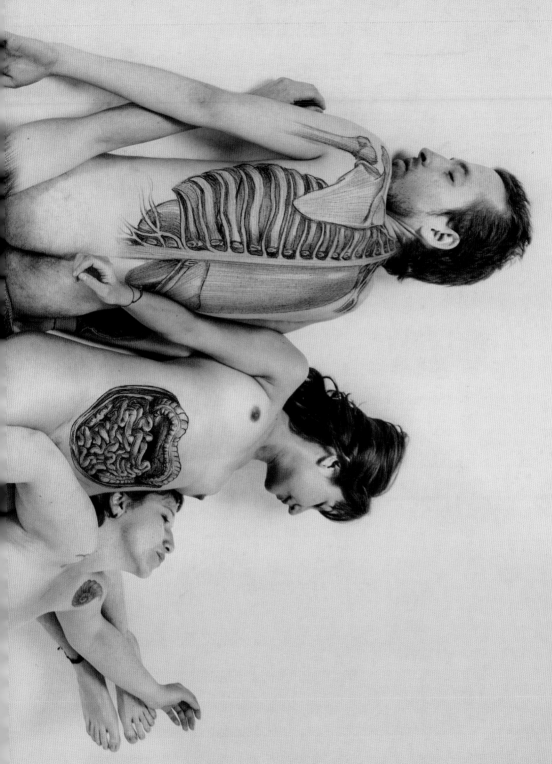

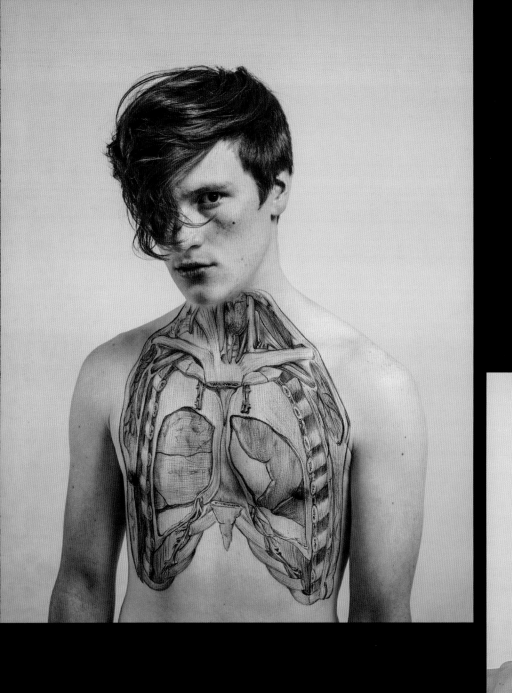

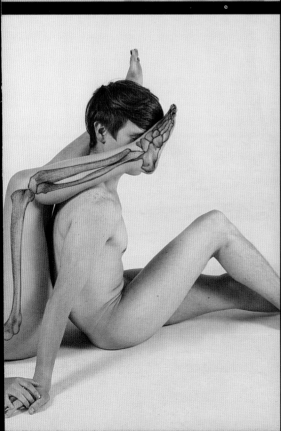

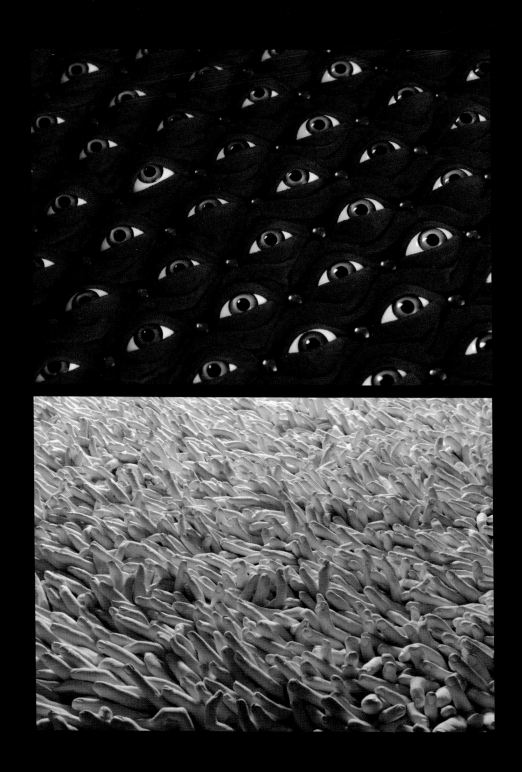

FIONA ROBERTS

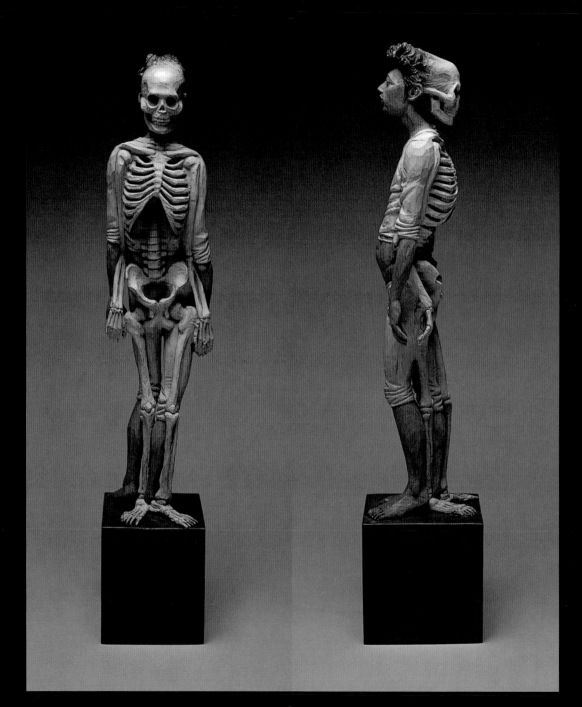

Round about the cauldron go;
In the poison'd entrails throw.
Toad, that under cold stone
Days and nights hast thirty one
Swelter'd venom sleeping got,
Boil thou first i' the charmed pot.

> Double, double toil and trouble;
>   Fire burn and cauldron bubble.

Fillet of a fenny snake,
In the cauldron boil and bake;
Eye of newt, and toe of frog,
Wool of bat, and tongue of dog,
Adder's fork, and blind-worm's sting,
Lizard's leg, and howlet's wing,
For a charm of powerful trouble,
Like a hell-broth boil and bubble.

> Double, double toil and trouble;
>   Fire burn and cauldron bubble.

[Excerpt]

Macbeth, Act IV, Scene I
— *William Shakespeare*

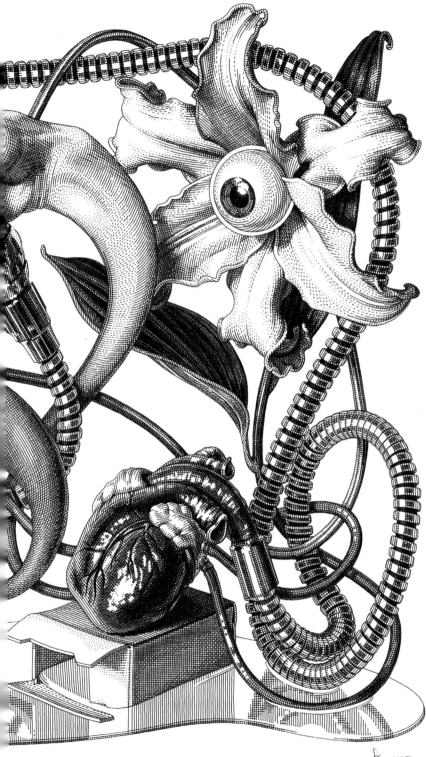

2015

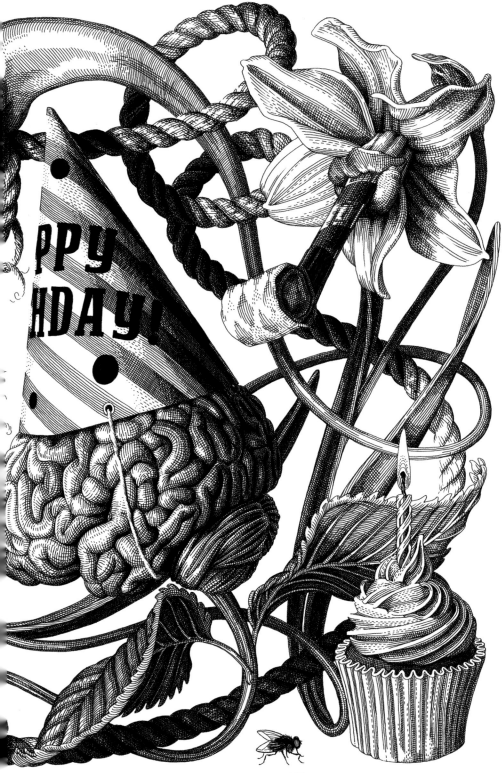

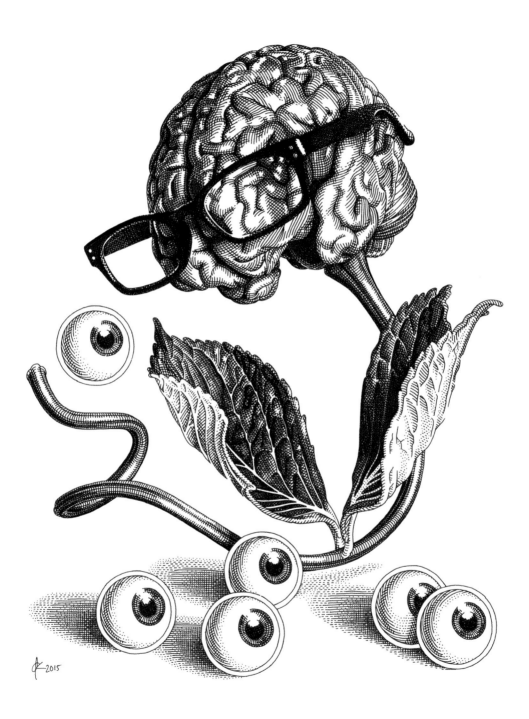

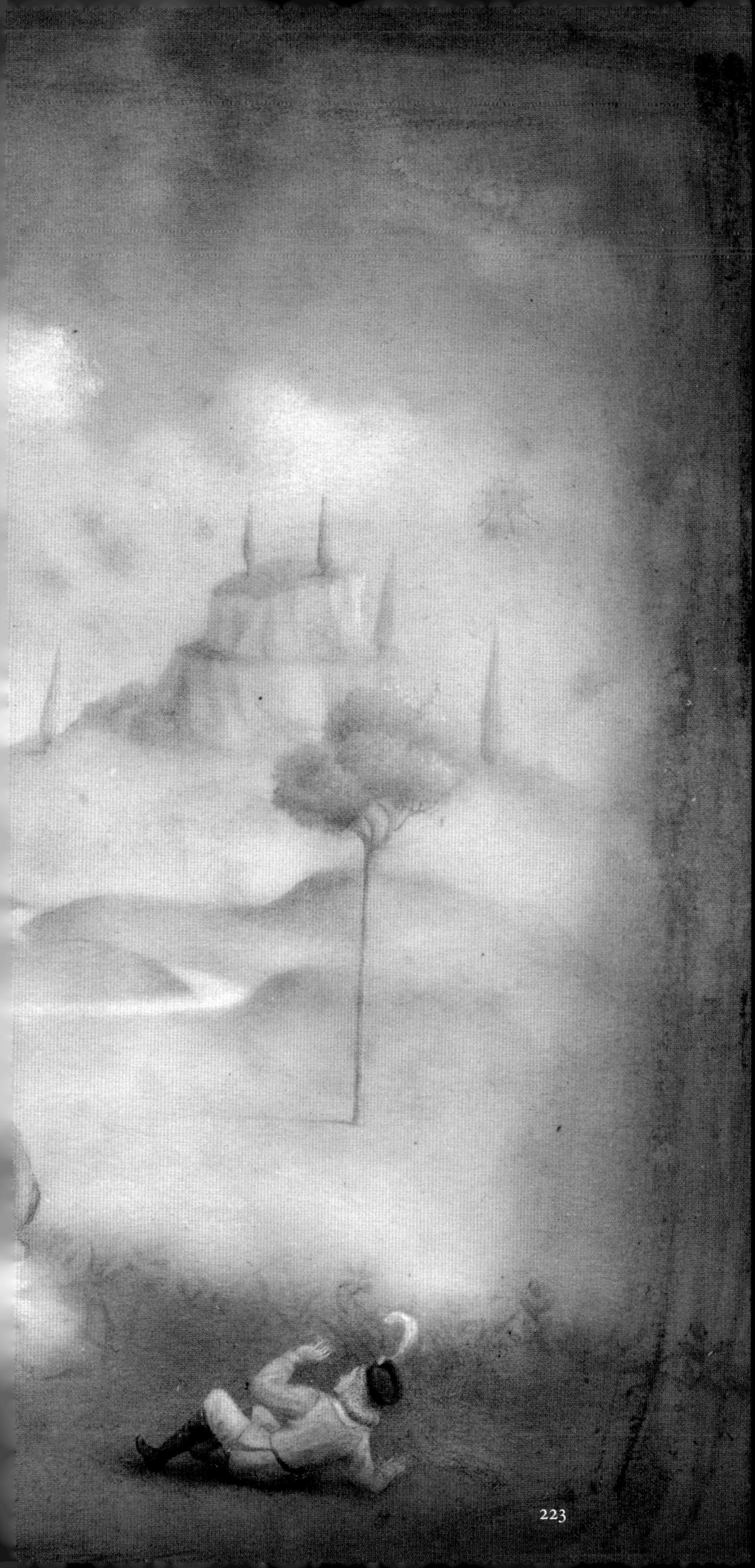

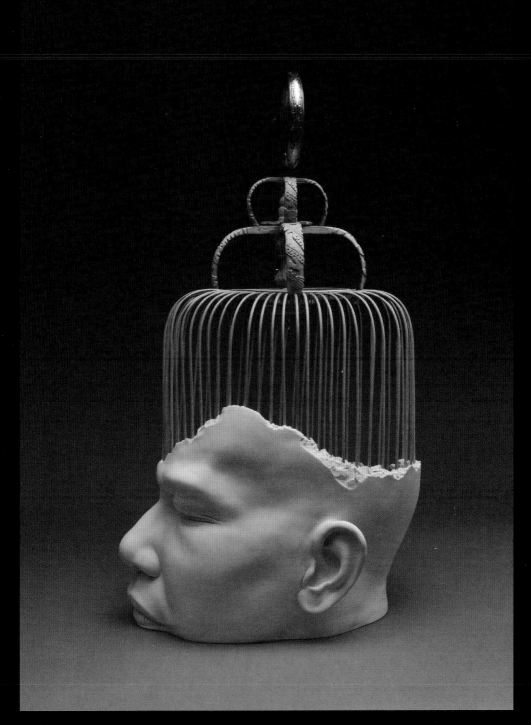

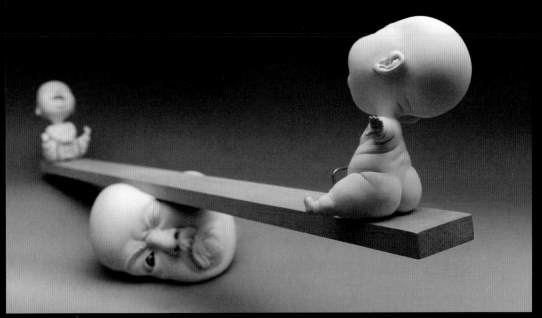

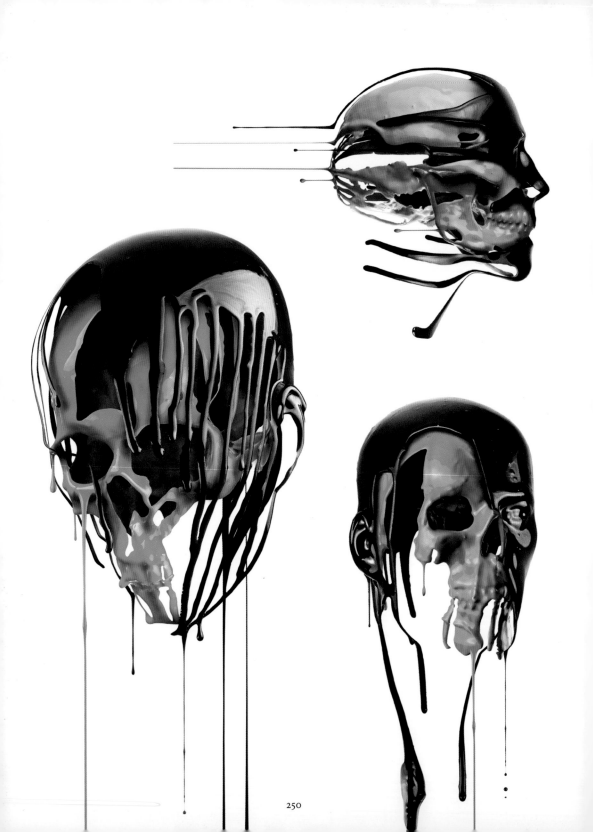

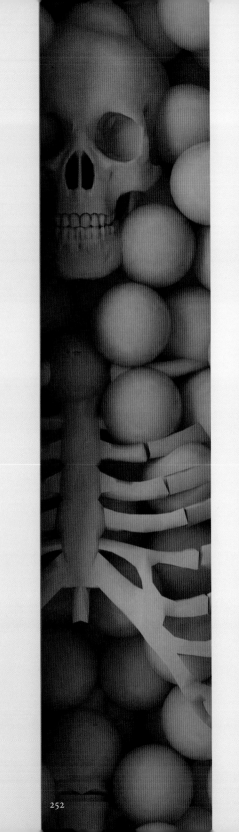

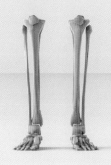

All attitudes, all the shapeliness, all the belongings of my or your body or of any one's body, male or female,

The lung-sponges, the stomach-sac, the bowels sweet and clean,

The brain in its folds inside the skull-frame,

Sympathies, heart-valves, palate-valves, sexuality, maternity,

Womanhood, and all that is a woman, and the man that comes from woman,

The womb, the teats, nipples, breast-milk, tears, laughter, weeping, love-looks, love-perturbations and risings,

The voice, articulation, language, whispering, shouting aloud,

Food, drink, pulse, digestion, sweat, sleep, walking, swimming,

Poise on the hips, leaping, reclining, embracing, arm-curving and tightening,

The continual changes of the flex of the mouth, and around the eyes,

The skin, the sunburnt shade, freckles, hair,

The curious sympathy one feels when feeling with the hand the naked meat of the body,

The circling rivers the breath, and breathing it in and out,

The beauty of the waist, and thence of the hips, and thence downward toward the knees,

The thin red jellies within you or within me, the bones and the marrow in the bones,

The exquisite realization of health;

O I say these are not the parts and poems of the body only, but of the soul,

O I say now these are the soul!

[Excerpt]

I Sing the Body Electric
— Walt Whitman

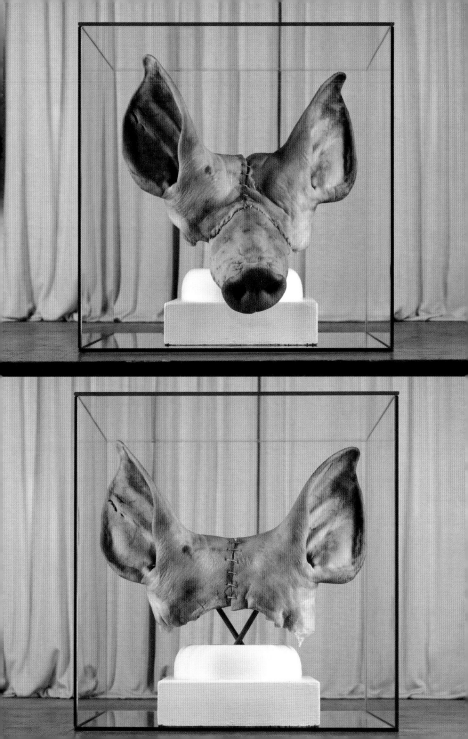

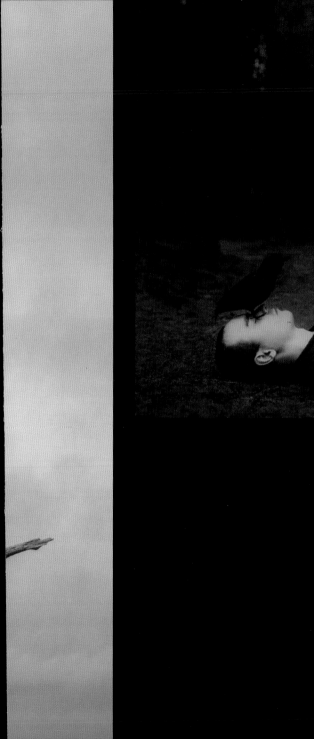

BIOGRAPHY

AITCH /

Inspired by her travels, naturalistic illustrations, naive art, childhood memories, legends and folklore, Aitch creates colourful watercolour artworks on paper, characters cut out of wood, painted murals and intricate patterns and illustrations for clients all over the world.

ANCORI, ELISA /

Born in 1990, Ancori graduated in Fine Arts at the University of Barcelona in 2011 and in Illustration at Bau University in 2012. Ancori's work has been exhibited in Barcelona, Paris and Germany, in galleries such as MISCEL-ANEA, Mutuo, Lafutura, and art fairs like GMAC and KÖLNER LISTE. Today Ancori is dedicated to artistic productions and free-lance illustrations in advertising, fashion and publishing such as Seix Barral.

BENCICOVA, EVELYN /

Born in 1992, Bencicova is a visual creative working mostly with digital photography. Grew up in Bratislava, Slovakia and after a career in modelling, the artist turned to the creative field and is currently studying photography and fine art at the University of Applied Arts in Vienna. Bencicova works towards where the commercial and artistic creativity meet, focusing on the conceptual and the visual aspect of photography, bringing out strong messages that are actively communicated with audiences.

BIANCHI, ALESSANDRO SICIOLDR /

Bianchi is an Italian painter and illustrator born in 1990 in Tarquinia and now lives and works in Perugia. His visionary attitude began to sprout in early childhood, depicting a strange and uncanny world, which brought a scared kindergarten teacher to call his parents, asking for an exorcism. He began with studying and working under his father's guidance on classical painting, and moved to his personal atelier in 2014. His work is often inspired by his dreamy visions and from studies of art history, psychology, mythology, philosophy, literature and science.

BRUNOTTI, FRANCESCO /

Brunotti is an Italian creative who focuses on motion graphics, music videos, photography and graphic design. He has worked with several agencies and a lot of international musical bands. Brunotti also creates personal projects, mostly about photography.

CARMAGNOLA, GIACOMO /

Carmanola was born in 1992 in Montebelluna, Italy. He started with illustrations and paintings. After studying graphic design and communication at university, courses on the use of graphics allow him to develop new styles completely different from the illustrations he had done up to that time. Recently Carmanola has been developing the technique of "glitch collage" for his work.

CECCOLI, NICOLETTA / *220-229*

Ceccoli is a freelance illustrator living and working in the Republic of San Marino. Playing with contradictions like the dark side of a nursery rhyme or a dream of lovely things with a hint of darkness, Ceccoli's whimsical yet disturbing work has been exhibited by the AFA gallery of New york in USA, Taiwan, Germany, Canada, France, and UK. Many of her children books have also been translated worldwide.

CHIBA, KOTARO / *138-140*

Chiba is a freelance illustrator who was born in Japan and lives in Niigata. He started printing his illustrations on T-shirts in around 2007 and later illustrates for books, magazines, vinyls and creates portraits commissioned from around the world. Chiba is also a graphic designer creating logos, branding, business cards, posters and flyers, etc.

DAINA, UMBERTO / *252-253*

Daina is a multidisciplinary illustrator and artist. Originally from Sicily, Italy, he now lives and works in Florence. In 2006, Daina founded Studio plus plus with Fabio Ciaravella and Vincenzo Fiore. It is an artist collective that takes part in numerous exhibitions in Italy and abroad. A freelance filmmaker and graphic designer, Daina has also been teaching 3D animation at the Accademia Italiana of Florence since 2011.

DE VITO, RAFFAELLO / *255-257*

De Vito was born in Mirandola in 1967. He began his career as a photographer in an advertising photography agency in 1981. He now lives and works in Reggio Emilia, Italy.

DIAZ, DANIEL MARTIN / *116-121*

Based in Tucson, Arizona, Diaz is a fine artist with an insatiable curiosity to explore the mysteries of life and science. His work has been exhibited worldwide and has been published in *LA Times*, *New York Times*, *Juxtapoz*, *Hi-Fructose Magazine*, *Lowrider Magazine* and four personal art books. Diaz has created artwork for large public art projects in the US and has won many awards such as a gold and platinum record designed for Atlantic Records.

DRØMSJEL / *122-129*

Aka Pierre Schmidt, drømsjel was born in 1987 in a small city near Cologne, Germany. He served an apprenticeship for an advertising agency from 2009 till 2011, and moved to Berlin then where he has lived and worked ever since. drømsjel's work floats freely between illustration and collage, traditional and digital. The artist splices vintage photographs of well-groomed ladies and gentlemen that evoke the standards of 20th-century propriety, turning them into bastions of surreal visions.

DUPRE, LOLA / *068-075*

Dupre is a collage artist and illustrator currently based between Ireland and Spain. Working exclusively with paper and scissors, her work references both the Dada aesthetic of the early 20th century and the digital manipulations of the present day. Dupre has worked and collaborated with Nike, Jordan, Penguin Books, *New Republic* magazine, *New York Magazine* and SUPERbrand surfboards among others.

FORLAND ISAKSEN, HÅVARD / *246-247*

Forland Isaksen is a Norwegian motion graphic artist based in Oslo, Norway. He is a diverse artist that uses a wide range of mediums to create his work.

GARANT, ALEX / *202-205*

Garant graduated in visual arts at Notre-Dame–De-Foy College in 2001 and has settled in Toronto, Canada ever since. Her work is exhibited all over Canada, the United States, Portugal and Australia. She is featured in publications like *Supersonic*, *Juxtapoz*, Mashable.com and many more. Garant's wet-on-wet oil paintings offer a graphic quality combined with traditional portrait techniques, where patterns, duplication of elements, symmetry and image superposition are the key elements.

HILLIER, DAN / *034-039*

Hillier has been working as a full-time artist since 2006. His work is exhibited in various established galleries including the Saatchi Gallery and the ICA in London; as well as solo and group shows in London, Paris, New York and Turin. Other than his own website and different exhibitions, Hillier's art can also be found at The Sunday Upmarket.

HOLLINGWORTH, PAUL / *248-251*

Hollingworth is an Edinburgh-based conceptual photographer whose fascination with all things photographic is born out of his love for graphic design. Blurring the lines between digital photography, design and art, his self-initiated work is often brought about by a natural curiosity for all things weird and wonderful.

HORAN, KATY / *018, 021-025*

Horan was born in Houston, Texas and received a BFA from The Rhode Island School of Design in 2003. Her work has been exhibited in galleries throughout the US and in Canada, published in several books including *The Exquisite Book* (Chronicle) and *Beasts!* (Fantagraphics). Horan has twice been selected for New American Paintings and was a finalist of the 2015 Hunting Art Prize. She lives and works in Austin, Texas.

HUMMEL, HANNES / *160-165*

Hummel is an independent multidisciplinary designer based in Cologne. He focuses on the intersection between new technologies and traditional design crafts to create outstanding experiences. With more than seven years of experience, Hummel has worked on a lot of exciting music and fashion-related projects in different mediums.

ISAK, GABRIEL / *270-273*

Isak was born in Huskvarna, Sweden. By creating photographs that are simple in form but rich in ideas and emotions, Isak's imagery entails surreal and melancholic scenes inspired by the world of dreams and psychology. He invites viewers to interact with solitary figures in his work that symbolise our own unconscious states, reflecting human experiences and the viewer's introspective journey. Isak is currently residing in San Francisco, California.

JOVANOVIĆ, NADJA / *109-113*

Born in 1983, Jovanović graduated in painting at University of Fine Arts in Belgrade, Serbia. The subject matter of her work is based on exploring aspects of existence — the presence of the individual in a moment and time, and self projection of realty. The epicentre of her work is the person, isolated from society framed in constant questioning of reality, in constant dualism of conscious and unconscious, closed in personal perception. The artist is now living and working in Zagreb, Croatia.

KANEMAKI, YOSHITOSHI / *206-211*

Kanemaki grew up in the Chiba prefecture in Japan. He graduated from the Department of Sculpture at Tama Art University in Tokyo. He loves origami, constellations and GUNDAM models since childhood. He mainly uses camphor to express the feelings of human being in his work. Represented by FUMA Contemporary Tokyo | BUNKYO ART, Kanemaki participates in numerous art fairs and his work is published worldwide.

KNAPP, OLIVIA / *214-219*

Knapp's tight cross-hatching technique involves long, slow, and steady curved lines that articulate the surface contours of her subjects, creating a supple and tangible imagery. These unswelled lines incorporate a "line-to-dot" rendering method as well as an extremely rare "dot-and-lozenge" rendering method that was used by 16th century masters. Her content explores the relationship between desire, reason, and circumstance.

KWOK, KAYAN / *088-093*

The founder of a k e k e, Kwok is an artist, illustrator and a graphic designer who has been living and studying between the UK, Canada, China and Hong Kong. Vintage, retro, pin up, collage are the keywords of Kwok's work. She is also fascinated by advertisments in America from 1920 to 1960.

LAMPINEN, EERO / *141-145*

Lampinen is a Helsinki-based illustrator who works with ink, brushes, watercolour and an eerie digital colour palette. His work is an intriguing blend of folklore and pop culture, often depicting offbeat characters in adjacent realities. Sugarcoated hues and modern decorative details paint the tone for these dreamlike scenarios that blur the lines between fantasy and reality.

LIN, ALICE / *146-147*

Born in 1980 and lives in Beijing, Lin is a freelance painter, illustrator and 3D-effects artist. She began studying calligraphy, Chinese painting and classical poetry when she was a child. Her style is rich and full of details, integrating watercolour and several Chinese techniques to express a unique, weird and fanciful wonderland that reveals the universe of mind and emotions.

MAGDALENO, MARIANA / *134-137*

The discovery of identity, spiritual nature, mimesis between animals and humans, as well as the hybridisation between good and evil are recurring themes in Magdaleno's work. She has been involved in contemporary art fairs in Italy, Argentina, USA, Canada and Belgium, as well as various exhibitions in Mexico. The Grant winner of the Youth programme of FONCA Creators in 2010/2011 and 2012/2013, Magdaleno also manages FERAL, an exhibition, studio and permanent showroom of drawings in Mexico.

MARINANGELI, MARCO / *213*

Marinangeli graduated in 2013 from the Academy of Fine Arts of Macerata in Illustration and with honour from the ARS IN FABULA's master's degree in illustration. He is active in numerous art exhibitions and events such as the Fruit Festival and the Children's Book Fair in Bologna. Apart from working with publishers like Orecchio Acerbo of Rome and Strane Dizioni, he realised with other illustrators, the fanzines *Trekking* and *Eating* in 2014 and constantly collaborates with a group of artists known as UOMINI NUDI CHE CORRONO.

MEEKS, MIRANDA / *130-133*

Meeks earned a Bachelor of Arts in Illustration at Brigham Young University in Provo, Utah. She uses both traditional and digital mediums to create dark and strange illustrations.

MÉRELLE, FABIAN / *154-159*

Graduated from the Beaux-Arts, former resident of Casa Vélasquez in Madrid, Mérelle loves the shadowy world of tales and re-entered it by rediscovering his carefully preserved childhood drawings. Mérelle confronts a funny world referencing ancient myths and legends as much as major figures of art history or the tradition of anatomical drawing, sometimes with puns and quotes.

MIRALLES, JANUZ / *082-087*

Miralles is a Filipino visual artist who merges photography and painting to reveal scenes from his imagination. As elusive and cryptic as his works, Miralles creates fleeting but powerful emotions presented by monochromatic hues, bold strokes, and womanly shapes. His work has been exhibited in WAW Amsterdam and The Unit London, and have been featured in numerous publications. Miralles is also a writer of Philippine poetry, and slave to a growing army of cats.

MORA, SERGIO / **AGENCY RUSH** / *114-115*

Aka Magicomora, Mora's work is audacious kaleidoscope, punchy, mind-altering and colourful. He was born in Barcelona, where he studied La Llotja, and where he lives, paints, experiments, plays and creates. A multidisciplinary artist, his prolific work takes audiences to subversive worlds, with beautiful monsters and grotesque fantasies, in all aspects including paintings, illustrations, videos, comics and performances.

MORKOÇ, MERVE (LAKORMIS) / *094-097*

Morkoç's paintings are inspired by street culture and lives, where she feels independent. Enthused by animation figures, commercials and narrative styles of urban origin that surround her, the artist creates alluring narration and forms, while keeping a characteristic distance with the viewer. Morkoç was born in 1986 and graduated from the Department of Graphic Designs at Mimar Sinan Fine Arts University.

OPREA, RAUL AKA SADDO / *166-167, 169-177*

Romanian artist, illustrator and muralist, Saddo started his artistic career by founding one of the first Romanian street art collectives, The Playground. It brought him many projects for advertising agencies, as well as collaborations with galleries in Bucharest, Vienna, Berlin, New York, etc. Recently Saddo has developed his style into more elaborate shapes, with influences from old masters from the 15th to 17th centuries like Giuseppe Arcimboldo and Bosch, naturalistic illustrations, surrealism, religion, and mythology.

PEKDEMIR, TAYFUN / *058-061*

Pekdemir was born in Istanbul in 1989 and studied graphic design at the Trakya University Fine Arts Academy. He is now working as a freelance illustrator with special interest in street arts. Pekdemir has illustrated for international and local projects, magazines and children books.

PÉREZ, DAVID / *192-195*

Pérez is an illustrator and graphic designer based in Bogotá, Colombia. He is 22 years old and he excels in realistic portraits with ballpoint pen.

RABUS, TILL / *178-183*

Born in 1975, Rabus is now living and working in Neuchâtel, Switzerland with his work exhibited worldwide. All images courtesy of Gallery Aeroplastics.

REEDY, MICHAEL / *190-191*

Reedy's work has been included in over 100 national and international exhibitions and can be viewed in numerous private and institutional collections such as the Hoffman Trust National Collection in association with the San Diego Art Institute. He held a solo exhibition at Manifest Creative Research Gallery as well as small group exhibitions at Philadelphia Arch Enemy Arts and 111 Minna Gallery in San Francisco, California. His work is also featured in various magazines like *Creative Quarterly*, *Direct Art*, and *Hi-Fructose*.

ROBERTS, FIONA / *196-201*

Roberts' work focuses on the fragility of life and the discourse between the mind, body and home. She is a mixed media artist who uses a variety of traditional and non-traditional art materials including ceramics, digital imaging and oil painting as well as hair, furniture, upholstery and found objects. In 2015, Robert received an Australian Council grant to fund her solo exhibition Intimate Vestiges held at KickArts, Cairns, Queensland and Format Gallery in Adelaide.

ROHLMANN, BENE / *010-017*

Rohlmann was born in Münster where he received a diploma in illustration and moved to Berlin in 2010. The artist and illustrator mostly draws inspirations from surrealism, mythology, comics, cartoons, graphics of the first half of the 20th century, and his own childhood. Always filled with weirdness and dark humour, Rohlmann's work is featured in numerous national and international magazines, newspapers, on T-shirts, as well as in many exhibitions throughout Europe, the US, Australia and Singapore.

ROJAS H, PAOLA / *192-195*

Rojas H, 20 years old, is a young photographer of Bogotá-Colombia, her work is an exploration of elements that steals attention. She starts from curiosity for daily objects, through the body, nudity, colours, space and personal experiences that lead to intimate small narratives and catharsis.

SHIN, DADU / *054-055*

Shin is an illustrator living and working out of Brooklyn, New York. He attended the Rhode Island School of Design and graduated in 2010. His work has been recognised and exhibited by American Illustration, Society of Illustrators and Communication Arts.

SIMONSSON, KIM / *076-079*

Simonsson was born in Finland in 1974 and graduated from the University of Art and Design Helsinki in 2000. After spending three years in Canada, he returned to Finland in 2004 when he was awarded the Young Artist of the Year and was invited to work for the Arabia Art Department Society. Simonsson's work has been exhibited in private exhibitions all over the world such as New York, Paris, Berlin, Copenhagen, Stockholm and Helsinki.

SUŠANJ, ANJA / *056-057*

Originally from Croatia, Sušanj is a freelance illustrator currently based in London where she is taking a master's course in illustration at the Camberwell College of Arts.

TIÓ ZARRALUKI, GUIM / *062-067*

Born in 1987 in Barcelona and graduated in Fine Arts from the University of Barcelona, Tió Zarraluki's work is widely exhibited in Spain, Italy, Australia, Taiwan and Canada. He is also a popular speaker at different conferences and workshops in these countries.

TSANG, JOHNSON / *236-241*

Born in Hong Kong, Tsang is renowned for his ceramic and stainless steel sculptures. He was awarded The Secretary for Home Affairs' Commendation by HKSAR for his outstanding achievements in international art events, the Special Prize of Korea Gyeonggi International Ceramix Biennale 2011 International Competition and Grand Prize of 2012 Taiwan International Ceramics Biennale. He was appointed the Expert Adviser of the Hong Kong Museum of Art and the Hong Kong Heritage Museum.

UEDA, FUCO / *230-235*

Ueda was born in Japan in 1979 and graduated from the Department of Tokyo Polytechnic University of Arts Graduate School in 2003. Her paintings have won different awards in Japan and she started to exhibit her work since 2000, both in Japan and abroad. Ueda has published an art book *LUCID DREAM* in 2011.

URRUTY, AMANDINE / *040-049*

Urruty was born in 1982 and is currently based in Paris and Toulouse. After receiving her Master of Philosophy of Art in 2005, Urruty began exhibiting her work and working as an illustrator. Her illustrations have been exhibited in galleries throughout Europe, North America and Asia. She has published two books, *Robinet d'Amour* (2011) and *Dommage Fromage* (2014).

VAN RYSWYK, DANNY / *258-265*

Van Ryswyk works to produce paintings and 3D-printed sculptures of moody and contemplative characters, sometimes encased in glass domes, giving an eerie feel of scientific specimens from another era. Van Ryswyk's interest in the supernatural world began after an encounter he had with a UFO when he was a young boy. This event has led to the creation of a mysterious shadowy world for his characters.

WALISZEWSKA, ALEKSANDRA / / *050-053*

Waliszewska is a painter from Poland.

YIDO / *184-189*

Yido, for Yes I do Concept, is the pseudonym that Enrique Núñez uses to sign his works. Born in 1977 in Benicàssim where he currently lives, Núñez's work covers a wide range of fields including art and conceptual design, street art, graphic design, art direction, illustration, postmodern design, vector, character design, etc. He tries to convey different meanings through every aspect in his digital collages.

ACKNOWLEDGEMENTS

We would like to thank all the designers and companies who have involved in the production of this book. This project would not have been accomplished without their significant contribution to the compilation of this book. We would also like to express our gratitude to all the producers for their invaluable opinions and assistance throughout this entire project. The successful completion also owes a great deal to many professionals in the creative industry who have given us precious insights and comments. And to the many others whose names are not credited but have made specific input in this book, we thank you for your continuous support the whole time.

FUTURE EDITIONS

If you wish to participate in viction:ary's future projects and publications, please send your website or portfolio to submit@victionary.com